CRYSTALS

BY PATRICK PERISH

BELLWETHER MEDIA • MINNEAPOLIS, MN

BLASTOFF!
DISCOVERY

Blastoff! Discovery launches
a new mission: reading to learn.
Filled with facts and features, each
book offers you an exciting new
world to explore!

This edition first published in 2020 by Bellwether Media, Inc.

No part of this publication may be reproduced in whole or in part
without written permission of the publisher.
For information regarding permission, write to Bellwether Media, Inc.,
Attention: Permissions Department,
6012 Blue Circle Drive, Minnetonka, MN 55343.

Library of Congress Cataloging-in-Publication Data

Names: Perish, Patrick, author.
Title: Crystals / by Patrick Perish.
Description: Minneapolis, MN : Bellwether Media, Inc., [2020] |
Series: Blastoff! Discovery: Rocks & Minerals |
Audience: Ages 7-13. | Audience: Grades 3 to 8. |
   Includes bibliographical references and index.
Identifiers: LCCN 2019001633 (print) | LCCN 2019009547
   (ebook) | ISBN 9781618916440 (ebook) |
   ISBN 9781644870723 (hardcover : alk. paper) |
   ISBN 9781618917393 (pbk. : alk. paper)
Subjects: LCSH: Crystals–Juvenile literature. | Crystallography–Juvenile
   literature. Classification: LCC QD921 (ebook) |
   LCC QD921 .P4275 2020 (print) | DDC 548–dc23
LC record available at https://lccn.loc.gov/2019001633

Editor: Betsy Rathburn   Designer: Jeffrey Kollock

Printed in the United States of America, North Mankato, MN.

TABLE OF CONTENTS

RAINBOW QUARTZ

THE MIRACLE OF CRYSTALS

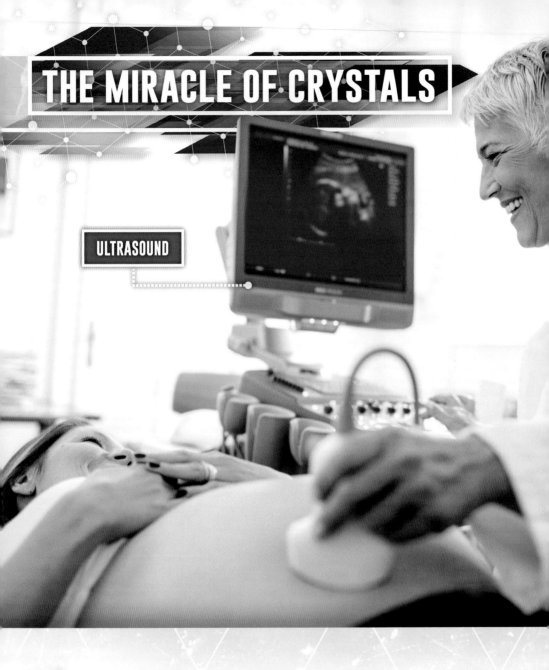

ULTRASOUND

At the hospital, a soon-to-be mother is having an **ultrasound**. The technician moves an electronic probe over her belly. It sends sound waves to a computer. On the screen, black-and-white images appear. The excited father takes pictures of the process with his phone.

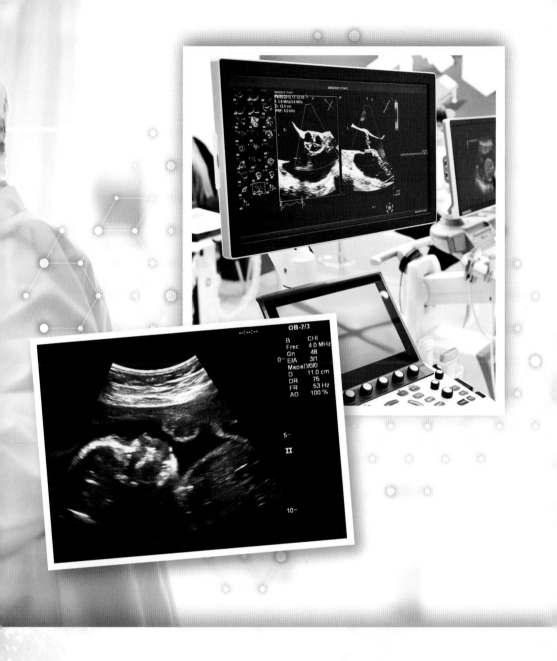

What do computers, cell phones, and ultrasounds have in common? None would be possible without crystals. These fascinating materials are all around us!

WHAT ARE CRYSTALS?

SALT CRYSTALS IN THE DEAD SEA

! DIAMONDS

Diamonds are a type of crystal. They are the hardest natural material on Earth!

Crystals are solid materials whose **atoms** are arranged in repeating patterns. They are found in every part of the world. Crystals include rare gemstones like rubies and emeralds. They also include common materials like salt and sugar.

Minerals in rocks are crystals. Snowflakes are crystals of ice. Table salt is made of thousands of crystals. Even aged cheeses contain crystals!

CRYSTAL PROFILE

NAME: QUARTZ CRYSTAL

HARDNESS: 7 on Mohs scale

| 1 soft | 2 | 3 | 4 | 5 | 6 | 7 | 8 | 9 | 10 hard |

TYPE: six-sided

FOUND: all over the world

MADE OF: the elements silicon and oxygen

USES: construction materials, watches, glass

Scientists identify crystals based on how they look. They may have flat **faces** and sharp edges. These shapes show the order of the atoms. **Microscopes** help scientists see this more closely.

Habit is also important. The habit is the shape of the crystal. Salt forms cube-shaped crystals. Emeralds are six-sided crystals! Other characteristics, like color, tell scientists what other materials may have been around when a crystal formed.

HEMATITE AND RUTILE CRYSTALS

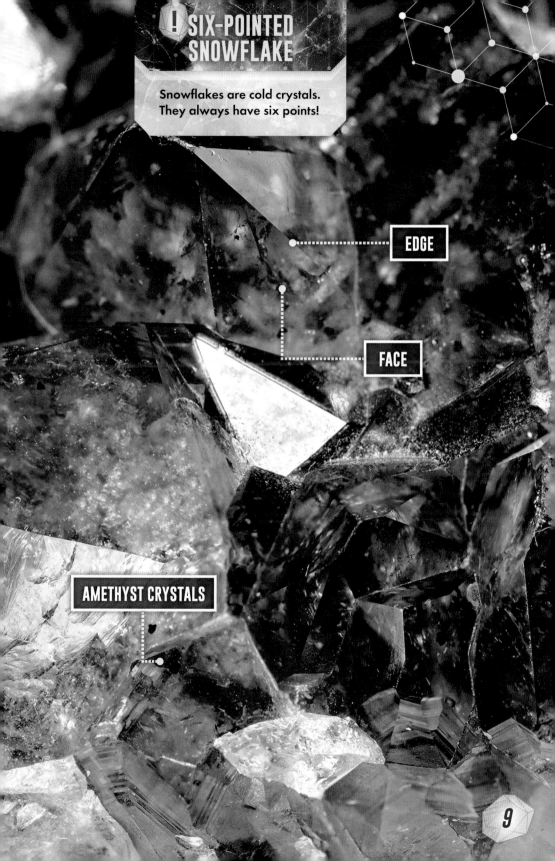

SIX-POINTED SNOWFLAKE

Snowflakes are cold crystals. They always have six points!

EDGE

FACE

AMETHYST CRYSTALS

Metals and most other objects are **polycrystals**. They are made of many individual crystals called **grains**. The grains join together at different angles. Some polycrystal objects, like steel, have a large grain. Other grains cannot be seen without a microscope.

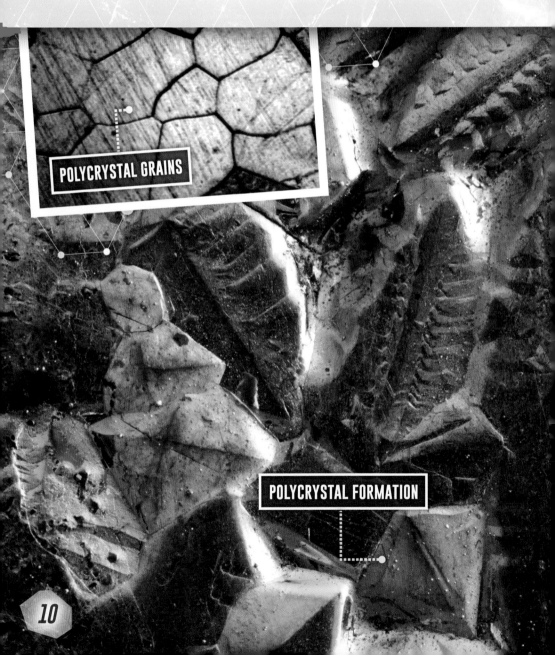

POLYCRYSTAL GRAINS

POLYCRYSTAL FORMATION

CRYSTALS IN THE RAUFARHÓLSHELLIR LAVA TUBE IN ICELAND

Crystals are everywhere. They are inside the earth and high in the clouds. They are even found in the human body. Some help keep bones and teeth strong. Inner ear crystals help the body keep its balance!

HOW DO CRYSTALS FORM?

CAVE OF CRYSTALS IN MEXICO

CAVE OF CRYSTALS

In 2000, Mexican miners discovered the Cave of Crystals. Its selenite crystals are the largest on Earth. Some measure more than 36 feet (11 meters) long!

Elements are the building blocks of crystals. Each element wants to act in a certain way. They combine with other elements to make **molecules**. For example, sodium and chlorine are two elements. Together, they make a molecule. They form the crystal salt!

As elements come together, they form a repeating pattern called a **lattice**. The lattice grows as more molecules attach themselves to it. This makes the crystal bigger. The slower the lattice grows, the larger crystals can get!

CRYSTAL LATTICES

CRYSTAL LATTICES CAN BE MANY DIFFERENT SHAPES. TETRAGONAL, HEXAGONAL, AND CUBIC LATTICES ARE SOME OF THE MOST COMMON.

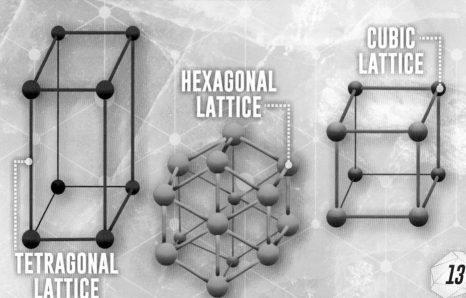

CUBIC LATTICE

HEXAGONAL LATTICE

TETRAGONAL LATTICE

Pure crystals are very rare. Most crystals have some flaws. Parts of the lattice may be missing. Extra molecules may squeeze into spaces they do not belong. This can lead to crystals in beautiful shapes!

RUBY CRYSTAL FORMATION

RED AND BLUE

Rubies and sapphires are beautiful varieties of the same crystal. Both are made from corundum. But impurities give each a different look!

An **impurity** occurs when different elements are introduced to the crystal lattice. Impurities are not always a bad thing. They can make crystals stronger. They can also change the way crystals look!

PURE FLUORITE

IMPURE FLUORITE

BUILDUP OF SALT CRYSTALS IN THE DEAD SEA

Crystals form in several ways. Some grow from **solutions**. Solutions are mixtures in which a substance is **dissolved** in hot water or another liquid. As the heated liquid cools, the substance hardens into crystals.

Saturated solutions must be heated up before they can hold more dissolved material. When they cool back down, they become supersaturated. Dissolved material may start to form back into solid crystals!

HONEY CRYSTALLIZING

CRYSTALS FORMING FROM A SATURATED SOLUTION

SUGAR CRYSTALS

Honey is a supersaturated solution. Sugars start to crystallize in old honey!

Other crystals form from **vapors**. Vapors usually change from gas to liquid. Then they become solid. But when air is cold, vapors change from gas to solid. They skip the liquid stage! The solid material may become a crystal formation.

HOW DO SNOWFLAKES FORM?

1 ICE SURROUNDS A TINY PIECE OF DUST IN A CLOUD

2 THE ICE FORMS INTO A SIX-SIDED SHAPE

3 EACH POINT BEGINS TO GROW AN ARM

4 THE ARMS CONTINUE TO GROW AS THE SNOWFLAKE FALLS

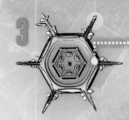

SULFUR CRYSTALS

Snowflakes form in this way. Vapor surrounds a tiny piece of dust and freezes. An element called sulfur also forms crystals this way. Hot sulfur gas rises from volcanoes. As the gas reaches Earth's surface, it hardens and crystallizes!

Crystals also form from melted rocks called melt. Melt can be made of many different elements. As melt reaches Earth's surface, it cools. The cool rock often becomes a crystal!

Scientists have found ways to grow artificial crystals from melt. In the early 1900s, a scientist discovered one way to make crystals by chance. He dipped his pen in melted tin. Thin crystals formed as the pen was pulled out. This process led to a method called crystal pulling.

CRYSTAL PULLING

1 SEED DIPPED INTO MELT

2 SEED PULLED OUT OF MELT

3 MELT PULLED UP AND COOLED

4 CRYSTAL FORMS

CRYSTAL PULLING

MELT

ARTIFICIAL BISMUTH

Today, crystal pulling is controlled by computers.
Machines dip tiny crystals called seed crystals into melt.
When the seed crystal is lifted, it pulls the melt along with it.
The melt quickly cools and becomes a larger crystal!

Scientists have found other ways to grow crystals, too. Crystals are sometimes grown on a flat base. The base is exposed to gases or liquids that crystallize. Other crystals are grown in special cylinders.

SCIENTISTS WORKING WITH CRYSTAL MACHINE

HOW ARE CRYSTALS USED?

SONAR MACHINE

!SUNKEN TREASURES

Sonar uses sound waves to find objects in the sea. Scientists have used it to study shipwrecks like the *Titanic*!

Crystals are more than just pretty rocks. They have many useful properties. Quartz crystals send out an electric charge when they are squished together. An electric charge can cause crystals to change shape!

This property led to the ultrasound. It also helped scientists make tools like sonar to find objects underwater. Quartz watches use this effect to keep time. Gas stoves use similar crystals to create sparks and light fires!

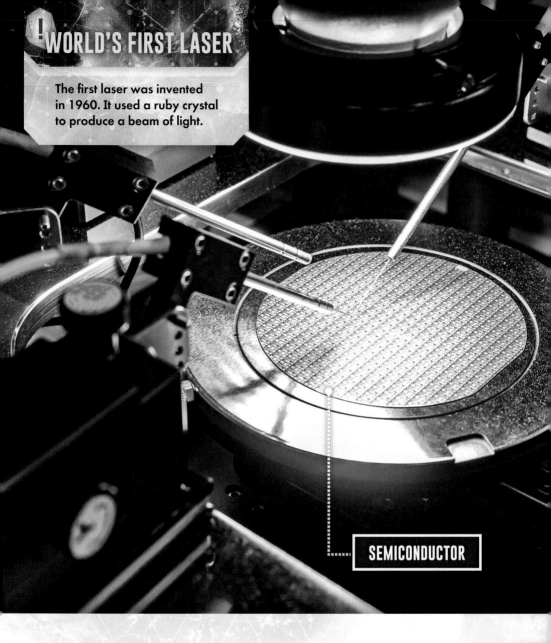

WORLD'S FIRST LASER

The first laser was invented in 1960. It used a ruby crystal to produce a beam of light.

SEMICONDUCTOR

The most important use of crystals is in our electronic devices. **Semiconductors** are made of crystals. They are found in everything from computers to rice cookers.

Semiconductor technology makes it possible for solar panels to capture light energy. In LED light bulbs, it provides long-lasting lighting. Semiconductors are also used in lasers and in bar code scanning devices.

GROW YOUR OWN CRYSTALS

MATERIALS

- 1 CUP WATER
- 3 CUPS GRANULATED SUGAR
- GLASS JAR
- PENCIL
- STRING

SUGAR CRYSTAL

DIRECTIONS

1 With an adult, boil 1 cup of water.

2 Add 3 cups of sugar to the water. Stir it in.

3 Pour the solution into a glass jar.

4 Tie the string to the pencil. Place the pencil over the jar so the string is covered in the solution.

5 Watch sugar crystals grow! They will get larger over several days.

LASER CUTTER

PENCIL LEAD

Most people use crystals every day. Pencil lead and drywall are everyday objects that contain crystals. Televisions, cell phones, and computers contain crystals, too!

Crystals are powerful tools with many uses. They help scientists study chemistry in action. They fall to the ground as beautiful snowflakes. New ways of using them are discovered all the time. Crystals are all around us!

GLOSSARY

artificial—made by humans

atoms—the smallest parts of an element that can exist

crystal pulling—a process for growing crystals by lifting them from molten material

dissolved—mixed into a solution such as water

elements—basic materials made up of atoms

faces—the flat surfaces on a crystal

grains—individual crystals that form together to make polycrystals

habit—the overall shape of a crystal

impurity—the presence of foreign atoms in a crystal's lattice pattern

lattice—a repeating structured pattern of atoms or molecules

microscopes—tools used by scientists to look closely at rocks, minerals, or other materials

minerals—materials that make up crystals

molecules—parts of a substance that contain one or more atoms

polycrystals—materials made up of many small single crystals

saturated—containing as much dissolved material as can be stably held

semiconductors—solid materials made up of crystals that can conduct electricity

solutions—mixtures in which one substance is dissolved in another

supersaturated—containing more dissolved material than can be stably held

ultrasound—a technology that uses sound waves to create images, often used in healthcare

vapors—materials made of gases that float in the air; smoke and fog are examples of vapors.

TO LEARN MORE

AT THE LIBRARY

Leavitt, Amie Jane. *The Science Behind Wonders of the Earth: Cave Crystals, Balancing Rocks, and Snow Donuts.* North Mankato, Minn.: Capstone Press, 2017.

Perish, Patrick. *Gemstones.* Minneapolis, Minn.: Bellwether Media, 2020.

Spilsbury, Richard. *Crystals.* New York, N.Y.: Power Kids Press/Rosen, 2016.

ON THE WEB

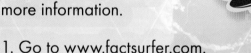

FACTSURFER

Factsurfer.com gives you a safe, fun way to find more information.

1. Go to www.factsurfer.com.

2. Enter "crystals" into the search box and click 🔍.

3. Select your book cover to see a list of related web sites.

VIVIANITE CRYSTAL

INDEX